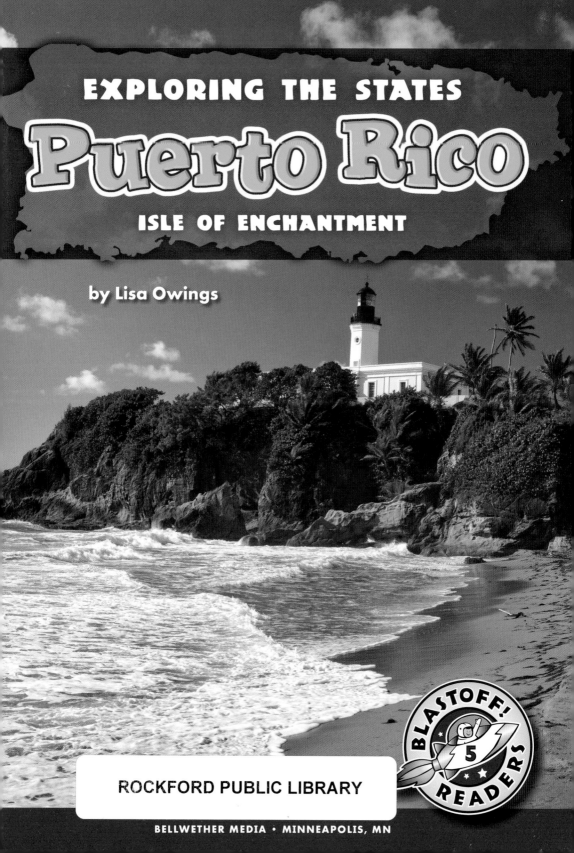

EXPLORING THE STATES
Puerto Rico
ISLE OF ENCHANTMENT

by Lisa Owings

BLASTOFF! 5 READERS

BELLWETHER MEDIA • MINNEAPOLIS, MN

Note to Librarians, Teachers, and Parents:

Blastoff! Readers are carefully developed by literacy experts and combine standards-based content with developmentally appropriate text.

Level 1 provides the most support through repetition of high-frequency words, light text, predictable sentence patterns, and strong visual support.

Level 2 offers early readers a bit more challenge through varied simple sentences, increased text load, and less repetition of high-frequency words.

Level 3 advances early-fluent readers toward fluency through increased text and concept load, less reliance on visuals, longer sentences, and more literary language.

Level 4 builds reading stamina by providing more text per page, increased use of punctuation, greater variation in sentence patterns, and increasingly challenging vocabulary.

Level 5 encourages children to move from "learning to read" to "reading to learn" by providing even more text, varied writing styles, and less familiar topics.

Whichever book is right for your reader, Blastoff! Readers are the perfect books to build confidence and encourage a love of reading that will last a lifetime!

This edition first published in 2014 by Bellwether Media, Inc.

No part of this publication may be reproduced in whole or in part without written permission of the publisher. For information regarding permission, write to Bellwether Media, Inc., Attention: Permissions Department, 5357 Penn Avenue South, Minneapolis, MN 55419.

Library of Congress Cataloging-in-Publication Data

Owings, Lisa.
  Puerto Rico / by Lisa Owings.
     pages cm. – (Blastoff! readers. Exploring the states)
Includes bibliographical references and index.
  Summary: "Developed by literacy experts for students in grades three through seven, this book introduces young readers to the geography and culture of Puerto Rico"–Provided by publisher.
  ISBN 978-1-62617-038-4 (hardcover : alk. paper)
  1. Puerto Rico–Juvenile literature. I. Title.
  F1958.3.O85 2014
  972.95–dc23
                                                                    2013005980

Printed in the United States of America, North Mankato, MN.

Table of Contents

Where Is Puerto Rico?

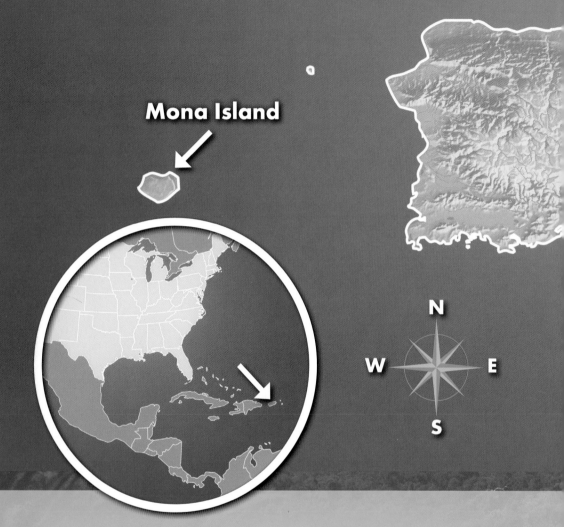

Mona Island

N
W   E
S

Puerto Rico is a **territory** of the United States. This **tropical** island lies about 1,000 miles (1,600 kilometers) southeast of Florida. Most of it is surrounded by the warm waters of the Caribbean Sea. Atlantic Ocean waves pound the northern coast. The island's capital city of San Juan overlooks the Atlantic.

Atlantic Ocean

San Juan

Culebra

Bayamón

Carolina

Puerto Rico

El Yunque
National
Forest

Vieques

Ponce

Did you know?
Puerto Rico means "rich port" in Spanish. Spanish and English are the island's official languages.

Caribbean Sea

Puerto Rico is part of a larger chain of islands in the Caribbean. Haiti and the Dominican Republic share the island west of Puerto Rico. The British Virgin Islands stretch out to the east. Several smaller islands belong to Puerto Rico. Mona Island is far to the west. Vieques and Culebra lie off the eastern shore.

History

The Taíno were the **native** people of Puerto Rico. They lived there for centuries before Christopher Columbus arrived in 1493. The Spanish began to settle Puerto Rico in the early 1500s. They brought disease, **slavery**, and war to the island. Puerto Rico remained under Spanish rule for nearly 400 years. It became a part of the United States after the Spanish-American War.

Spanish-American War

Puerto Rico Timeline!

1000:	The Taíno people are thriving in Puerto Rico.
1493:	Christopher Columbus arrives with seventeen ships. He claims the island for Spain.
1508:	The Spanish begin to settle Puerto Rico.
1898:	The United States gains control of Puerto Rico after the Spanish-American War.
1917:	Puerto Ricans are granted U.S. citizenship.
1948:	Luis Muñoz Marín is the first Governor of Puerto Rico to be elected by the people.
1952:	Puerto Rico becomes a commonwealth. That means it governs itself but is still tied to the United States.
2000:	Sila María Calderón becomes the first woman to serve as Puerto Rico's Governor.
2011:	Barack Obama makes the first presidential visit to Puerto Rico since 1961.
2012:	Puerto Ricans vote in favor of becoming a state.

native Taíno

Christopher Columbus

Sila María Calderón

The Land

Puerto Rico's Climate
average °F

spring
Low: 73°
High: 86°

summer
Low: 76°
High: 89°

fall
Low: 75°
High: 88°

winter
Low: 71°
High: 84°

Puerto Rico is a paradise of lush greenery and turquoise waters. Mountains rise from the center of the island. The tall peaks of the Cordillera Central stretch from east to west. Farmers grow crops in their **fertile** valleys. Rain falls in short bursts on the mountains' northern slopes. It forms rivers that flow into the Atlantic.

Northwest of the mountains are caves and other limestone formations. **Plains** line the northern and southern coasts. A ring of sandy beaches surrounds the island. Puerto Rico is warm year-round, but **hurricanes** and earthquakes are common.

! fun fact

Off Puerto Rico's northern shore, the land drops into the Puerto Rico Trench. This underwater canyon reaches the deepest point in the Atlantic, more than 5 miles (8 kilometers) below the surface.

El Yunque National Forest

El Yunque is the only tropical **rain forest** in the United States. Its misty **canopies** shade the mountainsides of northeastern Puerto Rico. Trails guide visitors past towering trees and bright flowers. Heavy rains in El Yunque create rushing streams and waterfalls. Hikers stop to cool off in the pools beneath La Coca and La Mina Falls.

High on El Yunque Peak, the forest is wrapped in clouds. The plants here are low to the ground and twisted by wind. Ferns and moss carpet the earth and cover the trees. Tiny orchids decorate this part of the forest.

fun fact !

El Yunque is known for its "air plants." These unusual plants do not grow in soil. Instead, they grow on other plants and gather moisture from the air.

air plant

Mona Island iguana

fun fact !

Mona Island is home to a rare species of giant iguana. The pointy growths on its nose look like rhinoceros horns.

Animals in Puerto Rico are small but varied. Each had to fly, swim, or hitch a ride to the island. Puerto Rican mammals include bats and mongooses. Iguanas and other lizards creep across the ground. The night air is filled with the coquí's song. The call of this tiny frog sounds just like its name.

Paso Fino
horse

coquí

Puerto Rican
parrot

Puerto Rico has hundreds
of species of birds. Some are found
nowhere else in the world. Puerto Rican todies,
woodpeckers, and screech owls are native to the island.
Only a few green-feathered Puerto Rican parrots still live
in El Yunque National Forest.

Castillo San Felipe del Morro

Did you know?

The Ponce Museum of Art boasts the largest collection of art in the Caribbean.

Puerto Rico offers both historical and natural attractions. The Castillo San Felipe del Morro stands guard over San Juan Bay. This **fort** was built in the 1500s to protect the city and its harbor. Visitors can see the cannons that once fired across the bay.

Trails in Río Camuy Cave Park take visitors through one of the world's largest cave systems. The Camuy River carved this underground world over the course of millions of years. Another natural wonder is Mosquito Bay on Vieques. Tiny organisms in the water cast a blue-green glow at night. Trails of light swirl around swimmers and kayakers.

Arecibo Observatory

! **fun fact**

The Arecibo Observatory is home to one of the world's largest telescopes. Its 1,000-foot (305-meter) surface helps scientists track objects in deep space.

San Juan

San Juan is Puerto Rico's largest city. Founded in 1521, it is also the oldest city in the United States. Old San Juan lies on a small island off Puerto Rico's northern coast. It is surrounded by protective walls. Behind them, narrow cobblestone streets wind through colorful Spanish-style buildings. Visitors enjoy the **plazas**, museums, and churches of Old San Juan. The Museum of the Americas and the San Juan Cathedral are popular sites.

The rest of San Juan sprawls onto the mainland. The heart of the city is full of busy factories. Resorts line the beaches, and cruise ships dock in the harbor. At night, the city comes alive with Latin music and dancing.

San Juan Cathedral

Did you know?

San Juan was once the name of the entire island, and the city was called Puerto Rico. Over time, the two places switched names.

Working

Most Puerto Ricans have **service jobs**. They serve the millions of **tourists** who visit the island's hotels, shops, and restaurants. They also work in banks, schools, and hospitals. Factory workers produce medicines, electronics, and clothing. These goods are shipped to the United States and other countries.

Farmers tend crops of coffee, tobacco, and sugarcane. Tropical fruits such as bananas and mangoes are also grown on the island. Many Puerto Ricans raise cows, pigs, or chickens. A small number of fishers cast their nets for snappers and lobsters.

Where People Work in Puerto Rico

manufacturing
9%

government
24%

services
62%

farming and
natural resources
2%

other
3%

scuba
diving

Baseball is Puerto Rico's national sport. Several players on U.S. teams come from the island. Basketball, boxing, and horse racing are also popular. The warm Caribbean waters are perfect for swimming, surfing, and other water sports. Snorkelers and scuba divers explore the island's **coral reefs**.

Locals and visitors enjoy hiking and camping in mountain forests. Bird-watchers hope to catch a glimpse of colorful feathers. Cities offer live music, dancing, and fine dining. At home, Puerto Ricans visit with friends, watch TV, and play dominoes.

Roberto
Clemente

fun fact

Puerto Rico native Roberto Clemente is remembered as one of the greatest baseball players of all time. His national pride helped Latino Americans succeed in sports.

lechón asado

frituras

Puerto Rican food blends Spanish, Taíno, African, and American tastes. A common meal features rice with beans, pigeon peas, or chicken. Soups and stews are also popular. *Asopao* is a thick soup made with chicken or seafood. *Carne guisada* is a **traditional** beef stew.

Special occasions call for *lechón asado*, or roasted pig. **Plantains** are cooked and served as a side dish. They can also be mashed with garlic to make *mofongo*. Flan is a classic custard dessert. Strong Puerto Rican coffee is served after most meals.

Mofongo

Ingredients:

3 unripe green plantains

6 ounces crushed pork rinds

1 tablespoon garlic paste

Vegetable oil

Directions:

1. Heat two inches of oil in frying pan to 350°F.

2. Peel plantains and cut into one-inch rounds.

3. Fry plantains until golden and tender, about 4-6 minutes.

4. Remove plantains. Drain them on paper towels.

5. Add garlic paste and plantains to bowl and mash until blended. Add pork rinds and mash until well mixed.

6. Separate into 4 portions and shape into balls or use a small bowl as a mold to make domes. Serve hot.

Festivals

In Puerto Rico, each town has a **patron saint**. These figures are celebrated with festivals across the island. The people of San Juan gather in June to honor Saint John the Baptist, or San Juan Bautista. At midnight, festivalgoers walk backward into the water for good luck. Ponce draws huge crowds during its February *Carnaval* celebration. Colorful parades and masked characters called *vejigantes* are highlights of the party.

Classical musicians from around the world pour into San Juan for the Casals Festival. The event honors Puerto Rican cellist Pablo Casals. The Aibonito Flower Festival takes place in the mountains. Visitors enjoy gorgeous displays of orchids, hibiscuses, and other tropical blooms.

fun fact !

Vejigantes are scary in a fun way. Their masks have long horns and sharp teeth. They playfully whack people with dried cow bladders as they move through *Carnaval* crowds.

Ponce *Carnaval*

The Taíno

Taíno helping Spanish settlers

The Taíno people lived in Puerto Rico long before the Spanish settlers. They called their island *Borinquen*, or "Land of the Mighty Lord." The Taíno welcomed the Spanish when they arrived. But many Taíno died from disease and poor treatment. Spanish and African traditions began to blend with the culture of the surviving Taíno.

Taíno carved stone

Centuries later, **ruins** were discovered at Tibes and Caguana. Carved stones surrounded plazas where the Taíno had held ceremonies and played ball games. Now Puerto Ricans work hard to preserve these sites. Taíno culture reminds them of their roots. It is one of many threads woven into the fabric of this island nation.

Fast Facts About Puerto Rico

Puerto Rico's Flag

The Puerto Rican flag has five alternating bands of red and white. On the left side is a blue triangle with a white star in the center. The star stands for Puerto Rico. The triangle and stripes represent the Puerto Rican government and the freedom of its people. The design was inspired by the Cuban flag and adopted in 1952.

National Animal
coquí

Nickname:	Isle of Enchantment
Motto:	*Joannes Est Nomen Eius*; "John Is His Name"
Commonwealth Founded:	1952
Capital City:	San Juan
Other Major Cities:	Bayamón, Carolina, Ponce
Population:	3,707,000 (2012)
Area:	3,424 square miles (8,868 square kilometers)
Major Industries:	tourism, manufacturing, farming
Natural Resources:	clay, stone, copper, nickel, gold

National Bird
stripe-headed tanager

National Flower
Puerto Rican hibiscus

Glossary

canopies—thick coverings of leafy branches formed by the tops of trees

coral reefs—structures made of coral that usually grow in shallow seawater

fertile—able to support growth

fort—a strong building made to protect lands; forts are often occupied by troops and surrounded by other defenses.

hurricanes—spinning rainstorms that start over warm ocean waters

native—originally from a specific place

patron saint—a saint who is believed to look after a place or a group of people

plains—large areas of flat land

plantains—banana-like fruits that are cooked before eating

plazas—public squares or open areas

rain forest—a thick, green forest; tropical rain forests lie in the hot and wet areas near the equator.

ruins—the physical remains of a human-made structure

service jobs—jobs that perform tasks for people or businesses

slavery—a system in which certain people are considered property

territory—an area of land that belongs to a country; Puerto Rico belongs to the United States.

tourists—people who travel to visit another place

traditional—relating to a custom, idea, or belief handed down from one generation to the next

tropical—part of the tropics; the tropics is a hot, rainy region near the equator.

To Learn More

AT THE LIBRARY

Muckley, Robert, and Adela Martinez-Santiago.
Leyendas de Puerto Rico: English and Spanish.
Chicago, Ill.: McGraw-Hill, 2009.

Rice, Dona, and William Rice. *Roberto Clemente.*
Huntington Beach, Calif.: Teacher Created
Materials, 2012.

Stille, Darlene R. *Puerto Rico.* New York, N.Y.:
Children's Press, 2009.

ON THE WEB

Learning more about Puerto Rico
is as easy as 1, 2, 3.

1. Go to www.factsurfer.com.

2. Enter "Puerto Rico" into the search box.

3. Click the "Surf" button and you will see a list of
   related Web sites.

With factsurfer.com, finding more information is just
a click away.

Index

The images in this book are reproduced through the courtesy of: Terrance Klassen/ Age Fotostock, front cover; (Collection)/ Prints & Photographs Division/ Library of Congress, p. 6 (small); Melvyn Longhurst/ Alamy, p. 7 (left); DieBuche/ Ridolfo Ghirlandaio/ Wikipedia, p. 7 (middle); Ramon "Tonito" Zayas/ Staff/ Newscom, p. 7 (right); Jason P. Ross, pp. 8-9; Wolfgang Kaehler/ SuperStock, pp. 10-11; hwongcc, p. 10 (small); Maresa Pryor/ Danita Delimont.com Danita Delimont Photography/ Newscom, pp. 12-13; Panachai Cherdchucheep, pp. 13 (left), 28 (bottom); Tom MacKenzie/ Wikipedia, p. 13 (middle); Jill Lang, p. 13 (right); Brett Critchley, pp. 14-15; Grecu Mihail Alin, p. 15 (small); SeanPavonePhoto, pp. 16-17; Greg Johnston/ DanitaDelimont.com Danita Delimont Photography/ Newscom p. 18; Associated Press/ AP Images, p. 19 (small); Specta, pp. 20-21; TSN/ Icon SMI 100/ Newscom, p. 21 (small); Katalinks, p. 22; Cpg-photo, p. 22 (small); Steve Manson, p. 23 (small); Luis Fernandez, pp. 24-25, 24 (small); Richard Schlecht/ National Geographic Creative, pp. 26-27; George Oze Photography/ SuperStock, p. 27 (small); Michael Roeder, p. 28 (top); Jose Oquendo/ Wikipedia, p. 29 (left); Tom Hadley/ Alamy, p. 29 (right).